SEEKING ORDINARY JOY

SEEKING ORDINARY JOY

A Poetic Journey from Restlessness to Happiness

DJ Murphy

La Quinta, California

Copyright © 2025 DJ Murphy

All Rights Reserved

ISBN: 979-8-218-60292-5
Library of Congress Control Number: 2025901880

First Printing, 2025

All rights reserved. No part of this publication may be reproduced, distributed, or transmitted in any form or by any means, including photocopying, recording, or other electronic or mechanical methods, without the prior written permission of the publisher, except as permitted by U.S. copyright law.

rehumanize
publishing, design & marketing

La Quinta, California
rehumanizebrands.com/publishing
Instagram: @seeking_ordinary_joy

Acknowledgments

"In the Chattering" and "War Wears Two Faces" first appeared in *Dulcet* (Winter 2025).

"Time Again" first appeared in *The Raven Review* (Winter 2025).

"Wind and Bear" and "What BBC News Couldn't Have Known" first appeared in *Last Leaves* (Fall 2024).

"The Book of They" first appeared in *Ariel Chart* (Summer, 2023).

I want to thank Peter Schireson for sharing his wisdom along my journey;

The Wordkeepers for inviting me into their inspiring poetry collective;

and my amazing daughters, Lauren and Chelsea, the earliest supporters of my dream.

To Sarah,
for her unwavering encouragement,
draft after draft.

Preface

This book is more than a collection of poems, it is a story, one that traces the emotional journey from restlessness and doubt, to healing and happiness.

Each New Year's Day we share resolutions to feel more fulfilled in the coming year, yet outside of big moments such as holidays and vacations and celebrations, life can feel like a series of *Wednesdays*—those moments in the middle of our true life lived—running errands; commuting; working; spending time with friends and family; being a caregiver; learning; overcoming loss; pursuing passions; questioning.

Joy exists in these ordinary moments, and on the other side of sorrow. It is this contrast that helps us feel what it means to be human, to find and appreciate that which makes us happy.

As Martin Luther King, Jr. said, *"But I know, somehow, that only when it is dark enough can you see the stars."*

This is a journey I have been traveling, and one I hope leaves footprints familiar to yours.

x

Poems

Chapter 1: Restlessness & Doubt   1

The Vanishing Point	3
Wind and Bear	4
Please Read Me a Story	5
Where Heaven Meets Dirt	6
War Wears Two Faces	7
Tell Me About Your Angel	8
Ripples	9
Hermetically Sealed Memories	10
The Weight of Curated Joy	11
Killing Time	12
Shattered	15
What BBC News Could Not Have Known	16
Never Fall in Love with a Building	17
What if the Asteroid Had Misssd?	18
The Calvary Is Not Coming	19
Skeleton's Day Out	20
Sun, Crow, and Wind	21

Chapter 2: Healing   23

Time Again	25
In the Chattering	26
Healing in the Grass	27
The Light of Being	28
Breadcrumbs	29
Time Before Time	30
The Book of They	31
I Need to be De-viced	32
Future Perfect, Present Tense	33
Grounded	34
The Stars are Curious	35

Chapter 3: Reopening 37

The Missing Puzzle Piece 39
But What Will My Dog Return As? 40
The Ordination of Identity 41
A Wakening 44
On Dark and Glittering Nights 45
Poor Wednesday 46
Small Spaces 47
Hummingbirds of West 52nd Street 48
Zipped Up Swaddling Fortress 49
A Confession, Kind Of 50
The Present 51

Chapter 4: Embracing 53

Seeking Ordinary Joy 55
New Year's Day 56
Limestone and Sea Sponge 57
Our Hidden Heart 58
How to Write a Happy Poem 59
Wrapping Paper 60
And Then I Hear It 61
How I See You 62
The Morning You Visited 63
Baby Hugh's Day One Orientation 64
Compass and Currents 65

About the Author 67

Chapter 1

Restlessness & Doubt

The horizon line stares back, unmoved by candles and wishes, curious why I cling to the shore.

The Vanishing Point

The horizon line stands still
in a shape-shifting world,

as do I this evening, staring
from the shore,

lighting imaginary candles, casting
prayer-like wishes to the wind,

echoes of twenty, fearing
my youth vanishing in the abyss,

and years later, a new father, hoping
my girls never set sail over its edge,

the place ancient mariners rumored
held the serpent's lair

and Renaissance painters anointed
as the vanishing point,

a liminal line separating
sea from sea, unknown from known,

unphased by forces that make
mountains rise and shorelines succumb,

now staring back at me, unmoved
by candles and wishes, curious

why I cling to the shore, when doing so
hastens my vanishing point.

Wind and Bear

       The woods are tricky,

a puckish maze
of mesmerizing beauty
punctuated by thickets of fear,

where pines turn wind
into words known only
to their roots

and choirs of leaves
exhale names of those
who stepped one step too far,

disguising under dirt and moss
the point where the trail fades as fast
as breadcrumbs tossed,

the backwoods kin of maples
that cradled me in tire swings
and two-by-four tree forts

now a shapeshifting foe
more shadowy than leafy woodlands
walked by Kilmer and Frost.

Which path should I take?
Which leads where I seek?
Will the crunching leaves wake
the hungry bear?

       The woods do not care.

Please Read Me a Story

Read me a story of Buddha
and Muhammad and Jesus,
tame the questions coiled within,
tell me a tale to make sense of
scriptures and science and chance.

Read me a story of America
and China and Ireland and India
and Comoros and Finland and Tunisia
and 188 other stories of wolves marking dirt
with the scent of dominion, without which
realms are rivers and rocks and flowers.

Read my story and I'll read yours,
singular books with similar beginnings
and arcs and endings, stories that
replace happenstance with purpose,
without which we are hollow husks
of flesh and organs and brittle bones.

Read me a story of humankind,
people on a pilgrimage,
a story of rocks and bones
and stars and rivers
and flesh and flowers
that will live forever.

Where Heaven Meets Dirt

Outside the motel
a sunrise school bus waits
to collect stick-figure portraits of despair

as nearby shadows
of Marlboro men ride Route 40,
their dusty dreams of cattle drives

now hauling
eighteen wheels to feed our
must-have-next-day-primal demands.

Miles beyond
the unfelt irony of the
Cheyenne boot store in Custer County,

Chief Black Kettle's
wound still bleeds at Sand Creek
while larger-than-life roadside crosses

furiously compete
with each other to save me
from myself as the sepia dusk of Route 66

slowly cloaks
this copy-and-paste landscape
of love and loss and hope and hurt,

a place in which
seeds of dreams work hard to take root
where earth meets sky and heaven meets dirt.

War Wears Two Faces

The day after the war
they packed the bombs in boxes
recalled drones to their nests
summoned tanks to silence their turrets

    and come crawling back

Refugees returned home to find none
fathers stared into the rubble of a school
ticking hatred took root in young witnesses
mothers suffocated from the smell of memories

    still clinging to clothing

The day after the war
people oceans away

    went shopping

networked at conferences
tried that new coffee shop
framed their child's drawing of their cottage
planted tea roses in the back garden

    to replace those that died

Tell Me About Your Angel

tell me
      about the angel
           who came

did she say
      if she's returning
           for me

or was it
      the bluebird in your
           olive tree

by chance
      did either mention
           my name

Ripples

Fruits and vegetables will vanish,
deprived one by one

of their daily dose of pollen.
Sunday brunchers will ruefully reminisce

about sausage-stuffed honey buns,
animals will struggle to find food,

bartenders will struggle to mix a Honey
Caipirinha with muddled limes and kumquats,

the cost of growing crops will increase
and make corn the new caviar,

scratchy throats will go un-soothed
by a cup of Chamomile tea with lemon and honey,

leaving our descendants to never know
the bliss of Danish Blue on a baguette

drizzled with warm gooey goodness
after the last bee dies.

Hermetically Sealed Memories

Grandmother's sitting room,
where time labors to breathe
and sepia strangers stare through me
from the mantel.

My brother's bedroom,
possessions preserved in amber,
a space where sadness never lived,
a conceit undone by the sound of absence.

My mother's final home,
jet-lagged mementos—Irish spoons,
Pakistani hookah—dad's slippers
set by the bed just like before.

My kitchen table,
wondering what will tether me to time—
weathered hiking boots,
Waterford whiskey decanter,
scribbled lines in an unfinished book.

The Weight of Curated Joy

Memories hang
from a rusted nail driven deep

through peeling paint
on a wall of time,

the silent anchor
working in shadows

to balance fact and fiction
against the weight of curated joy—

cottage getaways from late August heat,
ghosts of Christmas past,
bramble berry picking for that night's pie,
photos of faces unwrinkled by time.

Some nights a memory will shake
my walls and rattle stories out of place,

creaking like the floorboards
in that cottage not visited in years

before softly resettling
in off-kilter frames.

Killing Time

I

I am dreaming
I am on the Orient Express,

an odyssey etched in my mind
by Agatha Christie's pen.

My eyes dust off a nap
and sense I am not Venice-bound

but rolling Chicago to San Francisco
on Amtrak's California Zephyr,

a train Hercule Poirot—
Agatha's mustachioed sleuth—

seems to have missed
or is disguised as the backpacker two rows up.

I wish we were passing through
the outskirts of Paris

yet it's still Omaha, maybe Lincoln,
hard to tell.

I kill time imagining the train
is a time portal roaring back to 1904,

a time when trains moved mortals
faster and farther than ever before,

while washing down a ham and cheese
with screw-top wine—

its faux-French name paints
Bordeaux's left bank on Nebraska—

and wonder if we unknowingly
keep company with people from time portals

visiting from the future to relive
the joy of cruising country roads, windows down.

II

I must tell the conductor
my idea of returning to 1904 was a whim.

I would rather go to 1972
on the banana seat of my stingray Schwinn,

pedaling home for dinner,
my mother's meatloaf encased in mashed potatoes

accompanied by a salad of crisp lettuce
and tomatoes and radishes from my father's garden.

A second faux-Bordeaux is approaching,
as is Denver,

framed by the towering Rockies,
settled by hearty people in covered wagons

who stared at those imposing peaks
and declared these flat plains would suffice.

Most of my family have passed
yet haven't teleported to tell me everything's ok.

III

Backpacker man tips his screw-top wine
towards me, his toast of fellowship.

He looks familiar,
a distant cousin of a different me.

Trains don't pass through pretty postcards,
mostly tattered parts of towns we avoid when visiting.

I paid to see the rundown backside of Reno
and will soak it in

as I would a rusty river in Berlin
spied from my window on the Orient Express.

I forget why I took this trip,
Hercule Poirot is not here to crack a mystery.

Maybe I am he, aboard to unravel a riddle
of my own making—

why the feeling of stillness
leaves me unsettled,

why I feel I'm falling behind
when not moving forward,

why I worry the portal will close
at an unmarked destination and unknown time.

Backpacker-Me hasn't once checked his watch,
for him, it is whatever time it is—how odd.

Shattered

A lump of clay
earthen elements

blended with water
molded by little hands

fired in a scalding kiln
glazed to seal in memories

a loving cup for pancake breakfasts
holding coffee and cream and more

now welling my eyes with
the sight of shattered shards

splayed across the kitchen counter
reminding me of my fragility

how easily I am broken
the glue I misplaced

the moments lost
how fast sixty years fly by

with fewer to go

What BBC News Could Not Have Known

South Africa: Girl, 8, only survivor as 45 die in bus crash.
BBC News, March 29, 2024

A wrong turn
sent a bus spiraling
from road to ravine,
an unscripted ending
to an Easter pilgrimage,
four seconds of scalding fear
slashed through forty-five people,
except Lauryn Siako,
eight years old, sole survivor,
for whom four seconds floated
without destination or deadline,
recalling her mother's happy tears
as Lauryn boarded with her grandmother,
a soothing memory pierced by primal shrieks
which Lauryn imagined to be the call
of a Martial Eagle carrying the bus in its talons
to a safe place in the shade of a Jackalberry Tree,
she felt her body suddenly clutched,
perhaps the grip of a long-clawed Kalahari Meerkat
digging a hole in which Lauryn could hide,
yet the arms clutching her smelled like home,
arms that stirred the savory pot of Seswaa
with its aroma of fatty meat and onions,
arms that guided her to school each morning
and home in the afternoon,
as Lauren Siako's grandmother
saved the life of her daughter's daughter.

Never Fall in Love with a Building

tumbling bricks
weep and wail

        each assault
        by the ball

            creates space
            for chromium steel

    where once rose
    stone by stone

a love letter
to a blushing city

What if the Asteroid Had Missed?

Imagine for a moment it did not strike earth,
no blast ushering in sunless winters,
ushering out much of life.

Imagine nothing more than a near miss,
apex predators would still prowl the earth,
humanity as we know it would not exist.

No Moses nor mosques nor Mayan temples,
no divinity would visit that rapacious hell.

No art and science and philosophy,
to be or not to be would not be our choice to make.

No time for anything but outrun carnivores,
no time for that which makes us human,
no self-awareness nor empathy nor justice.

But the asteroid did not miss,
causing us to conflate fate and luck
and gaze with gratitude toward the stars.

The Cavalry Is Not Coming

No heroes
will crest the hilltop,
none will gallop
across the plains
to save us from being
an echo in history,
another epoch of humans
beautifully imperfect,
mercifully ephemeral,
who cannot accept
time is caressed
never held,
amusingly cock-sure
the future stops here,
as were Babylonians,
Maya, Roman Emperors,
and BlackBerry users.

Skeleton's Day Out

Maybe today
my skeleton will dance,
unzip its tight-fitting suit
and tango into town,
lose memories of muscles,
bow at the altar
of chance,
sip lattes in a café
and chit-chat about this
and that.

Maybe today
my weary bones will learn,
wander library shelves
as though trekking
mountain trails,
hear Romans and Huns
tell tales of epic battles,
stand still in a museum
as brush strokes open
cracks in time.

Maybe tonight
my skeleton will dream
of a life among Gauchos
on gusty Patagonian plains,
drink Malbec to nourish
thirsty marrow,
and come morning
come home
to the comfort
of its skin.

Sun, Crow and Wind

I greeted the dawn.
Though the sun was still yawning,
we shared a coffee.

Do you know the time?
Yes, said the crow on the fence,
it's less than before.

Which way should I go?
Does it matter, asked the wind,
truth treads many paths.

My three friends moved on
while I sat seeking courage
to walk beside them.

Chapter 2

Healing

*We will meet by the river,
ford its roiling current
to find peaceful water
and together find strength
in our ability to endure.*

Time Again

Wait by the river,
see coming clouds threaten
to fatten its swollen banks,
feel in your marrow it is time again
to seek higher ground.

Wait by the river,
watch the beaver gather wood and mud
to build its protective lair,
his haste a harbinger that it is time again
to shelter where wolves do not go.

Wait by the river,
recall when this verdant valley
was charred then slaked,
accept that the chain demands
we again know thirst.

We will meet by the river,
ford its roiling current to find
peaceful water in hidden eddies
and together find strength
in our ability to endure.

In the Chattering

Breeze-blown leaves
semaphore a coming storm,
flashing their light green backsides

while downtown streets
start chattering with arrhythmic raindrops,
nature's morse code,

its discordant beat
a metrical muse embraced by
a street corner beatboxer

dueling with Coltrane's
brooding sax sauntering from
a second-story window,

a jam joined by my fingers
strumming a cafe table, contemplating
the lack of cabs and my choice of shoes,

as the rain ripples
a child's boat in the fountain
like a ship wrestling a rogue wave,

the moment when
the weather's gentle acoustics
give way to its symphonic might

and force me to choose
to outrun nature or stand still
and be cleansed.

Healing in the Grass

Each morning on her walk
my dog falls prostrate on dewy grass,

an immovable wiggling weight,
one part Labrador, one part jellyfish.

People do this too,
a practice called earthing,

a belief that our body heals
while standing barefoot in the grass

absorbing earth's energy through
our naked soles.

Bailey is a bright dog,
surprisingly current on this trend,

though she immediately un-earths
whenever I say *biscuit*,

my bribe to stand and head home,
a bright dog indeed,

smart enough to see me
in perpetual motion,

to hear my mind
alphabetizing anxieties,

to lie down and show me how to be still,
echoing to me my words to her—

heal, *heal*.

The Light of Being

Every star in the sky will die,
unaware they no longer shine,
confusing the reflection in our eyes
for the light of their being.

As will the swan,
plumed in white meringue,
gliding across the lake
like feathers stroking silk.

As will the palm tree,
its fronds echoing the breeze,
memories of dragon-fruit mojitos
and lazy days in Belize.

So, too, my Yellow Lab,
stealing a nap so soon after breakfast,
the reward for a hard day's work
better reserved for late afternoon.

We need not a telescope to know
we are infinity's dust,
here for a nanosecond,
a flash of little consequence,

until we see
the knowing smile of a lifelong friend,
savor the juice
of a freshly plucked orange,
inhale spring
to replace what winter stole,

feel loved
for the first time,
and realize nothing in the universe
matters more.

Breadcrumbs

Such a waste of wood
    it would be to keep
        words penned within
            the Book's bordered page,
           never lifting the latch
        and give them leave
    to wander my thoughts,
each word a breadcrumb
    I might follow out
        from this dense forest
           in which I sleep
              and return to the garden
                  where once I dreamed.

Time Before Time

The rising sun calls the desert to life
as I sit and stare at the cream
swirling in my coffee,

a moment of stillness to thicken
my mood against maddening traffic,
a cacophony of demands, an inhaled lunch,

while my body, a mass of spiraling atoms,
spins through space on an orb of dirt
eternally reshaped by oceans and quakes,

its rhythm metered from above
by a lunar ball of dust,
two partners in an infinite tango
joined by billions of trembling stars,
a dance ignited by a solitary spark.

As I sip my gently-swirled coffee,
I question if it is stillness I seek
or to know what drew breath

before the spark,
before the universe began spinning,
in a time before time.

The Book of They

I am a prisoner of The Book of They,
echoing self-righteous speeches
by Star-Belly Sneetches,

free-basing coded drugs, braying
ones and zeros, drowning
in the dross of vanity's insanity.

Where went those dancing days of May,
before winter's odious words
honored and mongered untruths?

What if They set us free, you and me
face to face, could we—would we—
close the faceless Book of They?

"Star-Belly Sneetches" references a character created by
Dr. Seuss in his book *The Sneetches and Other Stories*.

I Need to be De-viced

I stalked my girls
when they were young
with an enormous video camera,
affecting the look of a war correspondent
covering the carnage of sugar-fueled
birthday parties and Halloween parades.

Yet how often had I captured the scene
but missed the moment—there but not—
isolated by a camera that hid my lips
while whispering *you've got this*.

I remain hostage to push-button vices,
a digital Stockholm Syndrome
that keeps me one click apart from intimacy—
texting instead of calling, emailing
a birthday card, inhaling the internet
from the divot in my couch.

And here I am, alone in this coffee shop,
headphones on—my do-not-disturb sign—
when I should share a kind word with
the man feigning a smile to mask his stress,
or let loose a kindred chuckle toward
the fully de-viced dad nearby telling
his daughter how much he loves her
third-place scarecrow costume.

Future Perfect, Present Tense

Awestruck faces gawked
    at the first transcontinental train
        as it thundered past their Nebraskan farm.

Mesmerized eyes fixed on
    Edison's bulb, a bright magic
        they did not know but knew they needed.

I long to feel how our ancestors felt
    seeing a telegraph manifest words
        from somewhere a world away.

When will such a future arrive again,
    one that excites collective positivity,
        not the present repeatedly recycled.

Until then I will gaze up at a plane,
    watch its white contrails airbrush the sky
        and appreciate hundreds of people

reading books,
    holding babies,
        staring out windows,

like our ancestors did on the railroad,
    yet now with artificial kale chips
        and canned wine.

Grounded

Do you recall
when I whispered my secret?
The one where I'm hovering,
looking down at myself, frightened
I might no longer be there?

I remember you
lying next to me, holding me,
telling me you would not let me float
into the moonless night,
that you would keep me there.

The other day
I felt a looming lightness in my feet,
fearful I might soon slip skyward
through threatening clouds,
alone.

But that didn't happen—
I looked down and saw my feet
were where they needed to be,
scuffing the earth, walking
arm in arm with gravity.

The Stars Are Curious

The stars are not silent
they ask about us
why we don't shine
why we're blue
why we feel alone when
we have each other
why we never returned
curious if we feel their light
in our breath
in our marrow
in our being
wondering if we know
how proud they are of us
their ancient dust

Chapter 3

Reopening

*To understand how it feels
to be a puzzle piece
in something profound,
out of reach, yet right there.*

The Missing Puzzle Piece

Northern Lights
Southern Cross
places that
connect me
to a time
before us
like mountains
ocean depths
desert sand
which help me
understand
how it feels
to be a
puzzle piece
in something
more profound
yet right there
in my eyes
spectacular
comforting
a moment
that assures
I matter
telling me
to seek joy
savor truth
and always
keep a fire
burning for
the small child
wandering
in the dark
as he makes
his way home

But What Will My Dog Return As?

My witchy friend,
a good witch, an avowed vessel
through which energy flows,
chats with my mother, one year deceased,
still bending a stranger's ear.

My Buddhist-curious friend
recites the cycle of cloud to rain
to cloud and so on, how the
cumulonimbus returns to balance
on the head of a woman in Benin.

Yet the space behind my eyes
conjures nothing, my past life
memory an unplugged TV
unable to air a new episode,
let alone a rerun.

My writer friend sympathizes
in his writerly way, telling me
he and I suffer from *vuja de*—
that strange feeling we've
never been here.

He lives life as though
it were the only cup of coffee
he will ever sip, savoring every layer
of its sweetly roasted caramel aroma—no refill.

While that sounds delicious,
if given a choice I want to return
as my dog who delights in this life,
splashing about in the lake like a child
reuniting with a long, lost puddle.

The Ordination of Identity

I

In a choice that shaped history
and could have caused Americans to sing
Vespucci the Beautiful at July 4th picnics,
a lone mapmaker penned on parchment
the name Amerigo Vespucci, an Italian sailor
said to have discovered the New World,
a choice not unlike mountains named for men
whose boots never scuffed a summit.
Who anoints these givers of names
to places possessing indigenous identity?
This question wanders with me in Montana
while hiking Hell Roaring Basin and Dead Man Lake,
wondering why in a state awash in glacial waters
only this stream nursing my sore feet
was named Cold Creek, a choice unchanged
by prairie pilgrims who followed.

II

Some people wear an ancestor's name, sequenced
by Roman Numerals, while others live life as Moon River,
a name that made Moon's parents smile while skimming
the Modern Guide to Baby Names.

I am David, a name of contradictions—the biblical king
of Israel and pagan king of Ireland—inspired by my
parent's faith or memories of the woolen smoke of peat fires
that warmed their youth.

Seamus Olin Murphy felt upon landing in 1950s America
that his name sounded too Irish, too straight-off-the-boat.
Seamus became James, Olin became J—a star-spangled
moniker JJ Murphy spoke through his thick Cork brogue.

My mother wasn't overly fond of her middle name—
Philomena, too twee—yet her destiny was defined by its
ancient meaning—courageous lover—exiting Ireland
hand-in-hand with the former Seamus Olin.

III

Are names chosen or
do they choose us?

Do they serve as a sextant
to navigate our sense of self,

conferring on us our identity
or simply identification?

Would the United States of Vespucci
have spilled its blood at Normandy?

Had the roulette ball bounced left,
might Everest be Mount Norgay?

Am I biblical or pagan,
Dawid or Dáithí?

As I soak my trail-worn feet
in Cold Creek's tepid summer water,

I am neither,
and I am both.

A Wakening

Winter's last breath has given life
to newborn leaves animating
the giant elm in my front yard,
a colossus ever-conspiring
with Michigan's lake-sharpened gales
to engulf my home.

I shed again my boreal fur—
sartorial armor against
winter's exacting indifference—
reorder clothing in closets
to affect my seasonal renewal,

watch hydrangea emerge on cue
to serenade my street with a duet
of lavender and violet,
smile as lenten roses repaint
this hotel art landscape with the grace
of a pink and cream Monet.

I watch this chorus of color unfold,
morning coffee in hand,
fuzzy slippers on feet,
slowly awakening
to the central plot of a play
I have attended every year—

that spring portends nature's rebirth
as well as its replacement,
foreshadowing the arc of my seasons
to bud, blossom, and gently fall,
making room on the branch
for the next.

On Dark and Glittering Nights

I am Dawid,
outlaw shepherd
seeking sanctuary on coastal plains of Philistine,
eyes drawn to the dark and glittering sky,
celestial embers marking my path home.

I am Daithí,
wind-reddened fisherman
sailing coastal coves off Kinsale,
cursing the stars for conspiring with Norsemen
to guide their longboats to our isle.

I am David,
fortunate son
watching a telescope inhale the heavens
like a black hole ripping open the roof
of this observatory,

pulling me out
to float through time
with Dawid and Daithí, random particles
rising to the same name spoken to the sky
on dark and glittering nights.

Poor Wednesday

Wednesday deserves an apology
for being treated as the weekly equivalent
of beige, neither here nor there,

as near the end as the beginning,
a checkpoint on our way to
a more interesting day.

I never raise a glass to Wednesday,
only its feral friends Friday and Saturday
and their living-our-best-life pose,

consigning it to errands and to-do lists,
always my acoustic guitar,
never the electric lead.

Yet that may be Wednesday's gift,
those quiet moments in the middle
of my true-life-lived,

a day to savor life's metronome,
because without a steady rhythm
my song goes unsung.

Small Spaces

Since the rise of cities
        in Eridu and Ur, we have
                craved that rare treasure—

        space

to recharge, to heal,
        to savor in private
                a moment within a book,
                      a guilty biscuit with tea,

perhaps ponder something,
        or nothing.

Poets of old strolled leafy glades,
        sat by swollen creeks,
              let nature's symphony conduct
                      their thoughts downstream.

The rest of us far from babbling brooks
        break rules in search of space—
                beds become meditation mats,
                      toilets double as reading rooms.

In my small apartment
        my space is an antique chair
                tucked by the window
                      where I close the curtain

to extend the gift of space
        to a young mother who sits
                on her fire escape each day at dusk
                      savoring a hard-earned minute of

                peace.

The Hummingbirds of West 52nd Street

The hummingbirds have faded, gone
is the charm that swarmed the West Side,
living days and nights defined by none—
bird nor bat, butterfly nor bee.

We flitted and fluttered that summer
after college—in the 24-hour deli
whose owner taught me to order in Creole,

the 8th Avenue subway
where the busker's echoing voice
was richer than his hat,

Columbus Circle
where the leopard-coated woman
called each pigeon by name.

Oh, how it felt to feel so free,
lifelong labels nothing but words
shed and shunned, no longer trapped
in transition, sipping life unabashed.

Our nest on 52nd Street now sits dusty—
the stand-up comic farms suburban grass,
Brown's guitar-shredding grad points at pie charts,
the punks of CBGBs play pickleball on Fridays,

while I scribble words few will read,
tales of days and nights defined by none—
bird nor bat, butterfly nor bee.

Zipped Up Swaddling Fortress

Lightning's flash and fizz unfurls
above the Joshua Trees, backed by a
moody bass note murmuring in the sand.

A coyote's satanic yelp celebrates
a ritual sacrifice, pack elders showing
young ones how it's done.

Snapping twigs kindle fearful thoughts
of a cougar's footfall, delighted to find
a tent in its dining room.

Tidy white-fenced houses feel worlds away,
unable to equal the warmth of this
one-man-zipped-up swaddling fortress,

like the one that cradled a boy reading
The Call of the Wild by fading flashlight,
more pages dog-eared than not.

A Confession, Kind of

Every child should ask
if other verses follow
sticks and stones may break my bones.
Had I asked when I was nine,
later lines might have warned
of threats more sinister
than branches and pebbles,
such as the church bell
that fell and broke my leg
as I played on it while ditching
Sunday school.

Yes, the creator of everything
takes attendance.

After traction, cast, and crutches,
I returned to church, scared as hell,
convinced the priest kept a calculator
beneath his cloak to mete out
the proportionate penance or falling object.
I used confession each Saturday
like a multiple-choice test to learn
how God divined that daft idea
for smiting my leg.

Yet how could I not covet
Bobby Mazer's ten-speed stingray
with its wicked-cool stick shift?
And while I did not keep the Sabbath holy,
I did pray with all my might
for the Mets to win the World Series.

It seems the creator of everything
is also a Mets fan, so we called it even.

The Present

Being present is exhausting.
I'm in the moment while writing this,
yet that line just slipped into the past

while ten seconds ago these words
waved to me from the future.

I am present…again,

my French Press is half-full, a picture
on the kitchen wall is askew, hummingbirds
outside battle for sugar water,

triggering a memory

of my friend Sue battling stage four cancer,
phoning to exhort me to retire and live
as she wished she had done, regretting

the time she no longer had to road trip
with Marty and her dogs without destination
or deadline.

I'm back…clutching tightly

another cup in my hands, interrogating
a map until it confesses dusty backroads
from Santa Fe to Moab.

Chapter 4

Embracing

I'm finding joy in simple moments I missed while chasing the amazing, yet here it is, smiling back at me from the cow face stenciled in my cappuccino.

Seeking Ordinary Joy

There is joy in a lone Primrose pushing
through ancient quartz, propelled by its will
to live in the light.

There is joy in a Saguaro Cactus and its
long-armed shadow standing side-by-side,
a bond renewed daily by a soft-hearted sun.

Joy lives in simple moments I missed
while fixated on life's imperfections,

yet there it is, hiding in plain sight—
a cloud shaped like Ireland,
the grapefruit my doctor says can kill me.

I feel it while watching a school bus
take children to learn how to handle
the dodgeballs that will fly their way,

or seeing a four-way stop sign orchestrate
a cadence of civility, like strangers
holding a door for each other.

Joy never gave up on me while I was busy
chasing the amazing,

it was always there, smiling back from
a full moon decorating the midday sky,
a cow face stenciled in my cappuccino.

New Year's Day

Window shopping
for a life, ready to dance
with the person inside
and dare myself to dare—
a gym joined,
injuries forgiven,
a first novel filled
with well-spelled lines—
knowing Monday will soon knock,
a new week, like the one before
and others before that,
this time prepared to outpace
the unforgiving hourglass
that buries time
and leaves undanced
last year's waltz.

Limestone and Sea Sponge

I am porous,
no different

than limestone or pumice
riddled with microscopic holes

that leak blood when I fall,
leak tears when I hurt,
sweat under duress.

Please do not ask me to be
as strong as a rock, to find
my inner steel.

I am porous —
wonderfully porous! —
no different

than sea sponge
or desert cactus,

soaking up that which
makes me human,

absorbing love to feel I matter,
knowledge to set aside myths.

I am porous,
no different than you,
no different than the earth itself.

Our Hidden Heart

Inside our heart
hides another heart,
not bigger or better,
just another,
and another within that,
just in case.
Each stands ready
to spring forward
and fill the void
when, not if,
the first one breaks,
when hope confronts mistakes,
when joy withers and fades.
And so on.
But then, unannounced,
the next heart appears
and the world brightens,
once again.

How to Write a Happy Poem

Visit your favorite café
savor a cinnamon swirl latte
gather together sun-soaked words

like Shrubby Monkeyflower
and Yellow-Rumped Warbler
corral your words in a cozy barn

shield them from wind and rain
cancel the morning newspaper
allow nothing to contradict

the warmth of the azure sky
knit tiny blinders to strap on each word
lest they look up and see an airplane

jetting to far-off lands
leaving the words to wonder
about truth beyond borders

give earplugs to one-syllable rhyming words
to muffle misleading metaphors and similitudes
hide commas and colons and periods

that might urge the words to pause and ponder
allow sunny stanzas to age into
well-metered psalms of celebration

do not inject poetic turns or twists
which might imply a different path beyond
the one paved with sunbeams and bubbles

Wrapping Paper

Do Nobel Prize Judges wince
when given a thoughtfully wrapped gift
reminding them they've long snubbed
the inventor who gave the world
ten seconds of wonder
ten seconds of childlike curiosity
ten times ten seconds cursing
a box within a box
nesting in a third
a joyful gesture
shared across nations
and my daughter
who mirthfully wraps
a fifty-dollar gift card
inside a flat-screen TV box
a custom fortunately rejected by my cat
who has yet to gift me his prized mouse
wrapped in festive yarn

And Then I Hear It

across the café, barely audible above
hissing macchiatos and caffeinated chit chat,
That One Song finds me.

Its melody lifts me like a sky-bound balloon,
its chord progression conjures memories
of moments when life moved melodically—

at your graduation party, the soundtrack
when a Vassar-bound senior kissed a wallflower
junior like he'd never been kissed before;

in my car while cruising past your parents' house,
nervously pressing play-rewind-play to find
courage to ring the doorbell;

in my headphones the summer after college,
our futures stuffed in backpacks on the Adriatic coast,
the last time I saw you.

It is the song I've long imagined swelling
in the finale of a save-the-planet movie
as the actors—who might resemble me and you—
start their slow-motion hero strut.

As the music ebbs, it lingers long enough to flash
a mischievous smile over its shoulder, like you did
the night we danced in the moonlight.

How I See You

Light shimmers off your body
beaming photons toward me

at the speed of light
particles of kindness and joy

penetrating my eyes
and sparkling across my retina

igniting light-sensitive cells
that turn you into electricity

sending signals across optic nerves
to inform me your image matters most

finally arriving upside-down
until my brain sets you right side up

gently placing us eye to eye
where we safely share our light

The Morning You Visited

Cusp of dawn,
kettle dry,
I did not recognize you
but there you were,
beaming from the bookshelf
when you should have been
rooting through my pantry for tea,
shaking your head at my lazy box of bags.

Your choice was clever,
appropriate
for a woman who inhaled mystery books,
arriving in the study
to illuminate a most particular lamp,
an Edison bulb set in a wooden block,
switched on and off by stroking
its adorning metal airplane
painted Pan Am blue,
the airline dad worked for,
the man with whom you exited Ireland,
the man you've missed for ten years.
I stroke the plane,
shut the light.

Next morning, you again
beaming in the study.
I summon the strength to speak,
our first chat since the weekend
when we buried you,
and thank you for letting me know
you're ok and I will be as well.
I stroke the plane,
shut the light,
and seal your final lesson.

Baby Hugh's Day One Orientation

Hello little one,
welcome to your life, such a journey
you've had to reach your parents' arms.
There is much to learn, more to do.

Like many, you may grow up feeling
that everyone but you knows the rules,
but trust me, we all are learning as we grow.

You will quickly grasp the essentials—
to prize family and friends and be nourished
by the touch of a caring hand,

to keep yourself safe and do likewise
for those you love—after all,
we are fragile bags of bones.

Yet the advice I want to share
might well hold the key to your happiness,
because there will come a day when
you wonder if you matter

and spend precious time pondering
your place among the stars, as though
that answer lies sealed in the heavens,

when it is right here, beaming back
from the eyes of those who love you.
It is then you will know that
those stars at which you will gaze

would trade their planets and moons
for the chance to be you, only you,
if even for just one orbit.

Compass and Currents

I have set a heading toward
the outer edge of me

my ship's bow coursing unruffled waters
sails devouring wind

free from the mid-ocean eddy that ensnares
delayed dreams

seeking a latitude where I need not
beware serpents

fingers-crossed flat-earthers
are wrong

and compass and currents will
gently converge

helming a sea toward the horizon
of a life well-loved

About the Author

Biography

With Bailey, somewhere along Route 66.

DJ Murphy's poetry has been published in *The Raven Review*, *Last Leaves*, *Dulcet*, *Ariel Chart*, and received the People's Choice Award from the Art Alliance of Idyllwild at its 2023 Imagery of Words Festival.

He is a guest lecturer at the UC Irvine Merage School of Business where he teaches the power of empathy.

He lives and writes in the Coachella Valley and serves on the board of the Palm Springs Writers Guild.

www.ingramcontent.com/pod-product-compliance
Lightning Source LLC
Chambersburg PA
CBHW051701040426
42446CB00009B/1240